Dominie
Chapter
Books

# Penguin Pranks

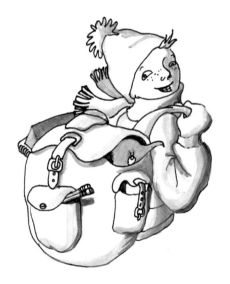

Written by Barbara Winter
Illustrations by Esme Nichola Shilletto

## DOMINIE PRESS
Pearson Learning Group

Editor: Bob Rowland
Author: Barbara Winter
Illustrator: Esme Nichola Shilletto

ISBN 0-7685-0744-8
Printed in Singapore
1  2  3  4  5  6  7  8  9  10  09  08  07  06  05

Dominie
Press

Pearson Learning Group

1-800-321-3106
www.pearsonlearning.com

# Table of Contents

Chapter One
**The Birthday Present**................5

Chapter Two
**P is for *Penguin***................11

Chapter Three
**Fish for Dinner**................18

Chapter Four
**A Very Long Morning**................22

Chapter Five
**Penguin Fever**................28

Chapter Six
**Penny!**................34

Chapter Seven
**Max Meets Penny**................40

Chapter Eight
**He Shoots! She Scores!**................45

Chapter Nine
**Penguin Cop**................50

Chapter Ten
**Penny Goes Home**................54

**Little Penguin Fact Sheet**................63

**Using a Dictionary**................64

Chapter One

# The Birthday Present

When Max and I got home from school on Thursday afternoon, Mom said, "Jake, a package came for you in the mail from Uncle Cyrus."

"Awesome!" I said.

Uncle Cyrus lives in Alaska and sends great presents, even though they always arrive late. (I'd already celebrated my tenth birthday just before Christmas.) One year, he gave me a box filled with cool rocks and fossils. For my eighth birthday I got a model spaceship, and last year he sent a box of magic tricks.

We dropped our backpacks on the floor, pulled off our coats and boots, and hurried to the kitchen to check out the package. It was a huge, rectangular block.

"I think it's a book," Max said. He's eight years old and

is really smart, although he eats and talks too much.

"Maybe not," I said hopefully. "It could be a game of some sort, about space maybe."

There was a row of stamps on the top. I tore off the wrapping carefully so I could save the stamps for my sister, Amanda, who collects them. The present was in a cardboard box with a card stuck on it. I opened the card and read out loud: "Happy Birthday, Jake. I know you will enjoy this book when you learn how to use it. From Uncle Cyrus with love."

I ripped open the box and pulled out a thick book. It looked very old. I turned it over to see the title.

"A *dictionary*?" gasped Max.

"A *dictionary*," I groaned.

"A dictionary!" said Mom. "What a very useful present."

"A dictionary?" Amanda asked as she walked into the kitchen. She laughed. Amanda is thirteen and usually she's pretty cool, but sometimes she can be awful.

"It's just what you need for school," Mom said. "I think Uncle Cyrus wants you to be a good student and learn how to use words."

"I don't need a dictionary to learn about words," I said. "I can find any word I need on the Internet at *dictionary.com*."

"Be grateful!" Mom said. "If you take care of that dictionary, it will last for many years and you'll learn a lot from it."

I went up to my bedroom, dropped the giant dictionary on my desk, and flopped onto my bed. I looked at the model spaceship on my shelf and remembered how I had really enjoyed building it with Dad.

I got up and took the box of magic tricks out of my closet. Inside was a wand, a top hat, a cape, a deck of cards, magic rings, a book of instructions, and a set of handcuffs. I grinned as I remembered the time I had used the handcuffs on Amanda. She was in charge when Mom and Dad went next door to the Hamiltons for dinner. She ordered me and Max around until we got tired of her. I tricked her into letting me handcuff her to the end of her bed. Boy, was she mad! Mom and Dad weren't very happy, either, when they came home. My handcuffs spent the next two weeks locked in Mom's desk drawer.

I heard Dad's car pulling into the driveway. I knew that

Mom would be calling us for dinner, so I went downstairs to the kitchen.

"What's with the long face, Jake?" Dad asked as soon as he saw me.

"Uncle Cyrus sent him a dictionary for his birthday," Max said, grinning.

"That's great, Jake," Dad said. "He must think you're smart enough to use one now."

"I guess so, Dad," I said with a shrug and sat down for dinner.

After dinner I finished my homework. Then Max and I watched some TV until it was time for bed. Max always has his shower first, because he's only eight. I went up to my room to wait for my turn in the shower. The first thing I saw was the enormous dictionary sitting on my desk.

Suddenly, a thought came into my mind:

*Maybe Uncle Cyrus tucked a surprise inside the dictionary!*

I lifted the book and shook it over the bed, but nothing fell out. Could he have glued something onto the pages? I sat down at my desk and opened the book carefully.

I noticed that there were pictures beside some of the words. I flipped through the pages to look at other pictures. Near the words starting with the letters *pe* was a drawing of a penguin. *Hey, that's interesting*, I thought as I tapped the picture. I moved the book closer to the lamp to read what it said about penguins. Just then, I heard a strange scuffling sound inside the closet. I turned around and listened, but it was quiet. I returned to my reading. Then I heard the sound again! This time, I walked to the closet and opened the door.

## Chapter Two

# *P* is for *Penguin*

Something moved among my shoes. Was it a mouse? I looked in the desk drawer for my flashlight. A little something scuttled into the far corner of the closet. I carefully aimed the light there and saw—a penguin!

My knees gave way, and I flopped onto the floor. I stared at the penguin. The penguin stared back. I shook my head hard, rubbed my eyes, and looked again. The penguin was still there, staring at me coolly.

My brain whirred like a helicopter's propellers, and my heart thumped crazily.

*How did you get into my closet?*

I reached inside to touch the penguin. It squawked and moved away. It was real!

*How did it get here?*

Suddenly I remembered! I had been looking at the picture of a penguin in the dictionary right before I heard the sound in the closet. Could this have something to do with the dictionary?

*What did Uncle Cyrus say in his card?*

"I know you will enjoy this book when you learn how to use it."

My heart thumped crazily again. Maybe this wasn't a boring old dictionary after all! Maybe this was an *amazing dictionary!*

Mom poked her head around the door. I shut the closet door quickly with my foot. Luckily, the penguin didn't make a sound.

"The bathroom's empty," she said. "Time for your shower."

"I think I'll have a bath tonight, Mom," I said, trying to keep my voice normal.

"I'll run it for you," she said. "Why are you sitting

down there by the closet?"

"Just thinking," I said.

"Well, don't think for too long. The tub will overflow."

As soon as I heard Mom leave the bathroom, I ran over, shut off the hot water, and turned on the cold water. I knew that penguins live in the freezing cold of Antarctica, and I didn't think this one would like a hot bath.

I threw a shirt over the penguin and picked it up. Luckily, it wasn't too heavy. I checked the hall to make sure it was empty. Mom was in Max's room, reading him a story, and Amanda's door was closed. I darted into the bathroom and locked the door.

Carefully, I unwrapped the penguin and lowered him into the tub. I was able to see him better in the bright light. He wasn't very big, only about the height of the bathtub. His back and wings were dark blue, and his stomach and feet were white.

The penguin was very happy to be in the tub. He flapped his wings and sloshed water onto the floor. He hopped onto the edge of the tub and slid into the water with a splash. I laughed as I grabbed some towels to dry the floor and the walls. Then I got into the tub. *Brrr!* It was cold!

Mom banged on the door and shouted. "What are you doing in there? You sound like a whale."

"Not a whale," I chuckled. "A penguin."

"Stop being a penguin, and wash behind your ears," Mom said. "It's time to get out and go to bed."

After our bath, I put the penguin back in the closet before

Mom came in to say goodnight. She pulled my blankets over me and bent down to kiss me goodnight. She sniffed hard.

"Do you smell something funny in here, Jake?" she asked.

"I don't think so," I said, and then I yawned so that she would leave.

"It smells fishy," Mom insisted, sniffing.

"Maybe it's from dinner." I yawned again.

"But we had chicken tonight." Mom frowned, switched off the light, and left, slowly shutting the door behind her.

*Whew! That was close!* The fishy smell came from the penguin, of course. I got out of bed and opened the closet door. The penguin waddled out and sat on my foot.

"I'm going to call you Pete," I whispered. He squawked. Suddenly, he started to pant as though he were hot. There was snow outside, but inside the house it was very warm. I had to keep him cool! *But how?* I scratched my head, and a brilliant idea came to me.

I crept downstairs and went to the garage. I found the cooler that Mom always used to keep our food fresh when we went on long road trips. Then I got the ice packs from the freezer and put them into the cooler. I carried it upstairs and put it by the window. Then I put Pete inside. He settled in and closed his eyes. We both went to sleep.

Chapter Three

# Fish for Dinner

When I woke up the next morning, Pete was on my pillow with his beak right by my ear. He looked hot and hungry. I checked my watch—it was only six o'clock, and the house was very quiet. I dressed quickly and took Pete downstairs.

I found some fish in the freezer and ran warm water over it to thaw it. Then I put on my jacket and slipped out into the backyard with Pete. When I put him down, he squawked, flapped his wings, and waddled across the snow. He was definitely happy to be outside.

I unwrapped the fish and put it on the snow. Pete hurried right over and gobbled it up. Then he blurted out a little squawk, which I took to mean *thank you*.

I was getting cold, but Pete was feeling right at home.

He waddled around the backyard, checking out his new surroundings.

When the lights came on in Mom and Dad's room, I grabbed Pete, tucked him into my jacket, and ran back to my room. I put him inside the cooler and moved it into the closet. I closed the door, leaving a little gap so he would have some air. Then I washed up and went downstairs for breakfast.

Dad, Amanda, and Max were eating cereal, and Mom was making a shopping list.

"What shall we have for dinner tonight?" she asked.

"Steak," Dad said.

"Pork chops," piped Amanda.

"Hot dogs," mumbled Max. He slurped his cereal, and milk dribbled down his chin.

"How about fish?" I asked.

Mom looked at me in surprise. "Good idea, Jake! Fish is good for your brain. What sort of fish would everyone like?"

"In batter," Amanda said, "if we have to eat fish at all."

"Fish sticks," Max said.

"I only want steak," Dad said.

"Just plain fish," I said.

"Right!" Mom said. "It's much healthier without batter."

"Yuck!" snorted Max. He tried to kick me under the table but hit Amanda, instead. She grabbed his hair. Mom told them to leave the table. Dad left for his office, and Max and I put the dishes into the dishwasher.

"Boys, don't forget you're eating lunch at school today," Mom said. "There are sandwiches in the fridge."

She looked inside the freezer. "That's strange, I was sure I had some fish in here."

"Great!" Max said. "If there's no fish, we can have hot dogs tonight."

"That's okay," Mom said. "I'll buy some fish on my way home. Hurry up, kids. I'll give you a ride to school. I have to go downtown today."

I ran upstairs to get my stuff. My brain was racing.

*What am I going to do with Pete? He can't stay here by himself all day! He'll have to come to school with me. Oh boy! He had better behave!*

I packed my books into my backpack. Carefully, I placed Pete inside. He did not protest. The tip of his beak stuck out through the flap. I hoped no one would notice.

We all piled into Mom's car. My best friend, Ryan, and his little brother, Brett, came with us. They live next door. Amanda sat in the front. She doesn't go to our school. Luckily, Pete stayed quietly in my backpack all the way to school.

Chapter Four

# A Very Long Morning

There are hooks by the classroom door where we are supposed to hang our backpacks and jackets. I didn't want to leave Pete there, so I placed my backpack on the floor by the wall near my desk. I hoped my teacher, a woman named Mrs. Simka, wouldn't see it.

I lifted the flap to give Pete more air. Ryan, who sits beside me, asked, "What's that in your pack?"

"Quiet!" I said. "It's a secret. I'll tell you later."

"Something stinks! Like fish," he said, wrinkling his nose and sniffing loudly.

"Shush!" I said. I was afraid the other kids would notice that there was a small penguin in my backpack. "I don't smell anything. You're imagining it."

Just then, Mrs. Simka walked in and called out, "Good

morning, class!"

As usual, she gave us a lot of work to do, beginning with math. As I was struggling with a problem, Pete wriggled and stuck his head out of the backpack. Ryan noticed him immediately.

"What *is* that?" he gasped. "Is it a bird?"

"As a matter of fact, it *is* a bird," I said. "It's a penguin. His name is Pete." I shoved Pete back inside the backpack before anyone else saw him. But Ryan was too excited to keep quiet.

"Here, Pete, Pete," he whispered. Pete squawked in response. Mrs. Simka turned to us. "Do you have a problem, Ryan?"

"No, Mrs. Simka," he replied. "Just a cough." And he coughed a few fake coughs.

When she wasn't looking, Ryan prodded me again. "Where did you get him?"

"I'll tell you at recess," I whispered. "Just keep quiet now, before we get into trouble."

♦ ♦ ♦

I was so happy when the recess bell rang. With Ryan's
help, I smuggled my heavy backpack out of the classroom
and headed for the far corner of the schoolyard behind
the gym. I placed the backpack on the snow and let Pete
out. He flapped his wings, gave a little squawk, and rolled
around in the snow.

Ryan's eyes popped wide in amazement.

"How did you get hold of a penguin?" he shouted.

I told him about the dictionary.

"No way!" Ryan scowled at me. "You can't get a
penguin from a dictionary!"

"I did, too!" I exclaimed. "I only looked at the
picture, and he showed up! Honest!"

Ryan shook his head. "That's amazing!"
he said. "What are you going to do with
him? He can't live in your room."

"I was thinking he could live in a zoo."

"How will you set that up?" he asked, as he went after

Pete, who had waddled off.

"I'll just have to figure something out really fast," I said.

We had a great time playing in the snow with Pete. We built a little snow hill for him and he had fun climbing up and sliding down, over and over again.

♦ ♦ ♦

The next period was music. Ms. Mills, our music teacher, is tall and thin like a pencil. She played some songs on the CD player for us to listen to. Then she asked us to sing. As soon as we started, Pete joined in with his squawking. Ms. Mills frowned and banged her pointer on the table. "Someone is really off key," she said. "Try that again."

We started again, and so did Pete. Ms. Mills held up her hand to stop us.

"I want to listen to each side of the room so that I can tell who is singing the wrong notes," she told us.

She waved at the far side of the class, and they began to sing. She smiled and said, "Wonderful!"

Then she waved at our side of the room, and we began to sing. Pete really liked the song. He joined in with some squeaks as well as squawks. Suddenly, Ms. Mills walked closer to me and Ryan. I dropped my sweater over my backpack. When she bent down to listen, Ryan began to

cough and sputter.
Ms. Mills banged
her pointer and
the singing stopped.
"Is it you, Ryan, singing
all those sour notes?" she
asked.

"I have a really bad cold,"
Ryan said in a hoarse voice. Then
he faked another big coughing fit.

"You'd better go and drink a glass of
water," Ms. Mills said, a note of concern in her voice.
"I don't think you should sing anymore today. We don't
want to strain your voice."

After another sputter of fake coughs, Ryan left the
classroom. The minute Ms. Mills wasn't looking, I shoved
Pete deeper into my backpack and tightened the flap so he
couldn't sing anymore. He fell asleep after that and was
still sleeping when lunchtime rolled around.

Chapter Five

# Penguin Fever

Ryan and his brother went home for lunch. I took the backpack and headed for a quiet corner outside again. I let Pete out and offered him a tuna sandwich. He pecked at it before deciding to eat it. After his stomach was full, Pete waddled around and enjoyed the cold weather. I watched out for passersby. Luckily, no one came to bother us.

When we returned to class after lunch, Mrs. Simka said, "We're going to the library now. Mrs. Lee will read you a story. After that, you can do research for your project on Egypt."

Pete was very still inside my backpack. I hoped he was asleep. I decided it would be safer to leave him in the classroom.

Mrs. Lee read us an exciting story about a submarine.

Then Ryan and I logged onto the computer and worked on our Egypt project. When we finished, I said, "Let's look for some information on penguins."

We found an excellent website that had pictures of penguins of different sizes and types. Pete didn't look like any of them. For one thing, he was much smaller than the penguins that were shown on the website. We scrolled down several pages, and then we spotted him.

"Look! That's Pete!" Ryan exclaimed. "He's a little penguin from New Zealand."

"Also known as blue penguins," he read aloud, "they are small, growing no taller than sixteen inches and weighing less than two pounds."

There was a picture of a little penguin standing beside an emperor penguin.

"It's just as well Pete isn't an emperor penguin," I said. "Look at the size of that thing. He'd never fit into my backpack!"

"I guess not!" Ryan said. "It says here that emperor penguins can be as tall as three and a half feet or more, and weigh up to ninety pounds!"

We learned that penguins can swim fast. They can dive deep underwater when they are catching fish. And they eat shrimp and squid as well as fish.

"You can ask your mom for shrimp tomorrow night and then squid the next night," Ryan suggested. I liked the idea of shrimp, but I was sure I wouldn't like squid.

Mrs. Lee clapped her hands to get our attention. "Okay, class. It's time to pack up and return to your homeroom for art."

Ryan and I rushed ahead to check on Pete. The backpack was lying open and empty on the floor beside my desk. Pete was nowhere in sight!

"Oh boy!" I exclaimed in alarm.

"Oh boy!" Ryan echoed, panic-stricken.

Just then, Mrs. Simka showed up. I moaned loudly and clutched my stomach.

"What's the matter?" she asked.

"I don't feel well," I said and groaned again. "I think I'm going to throw up."

"Go to the bathroom at once," she said. Walking bent over, I made a quick exit.

I ran down the hallway, peeping into all the open doors. There was no sign of a penguin anywhere.

Suddenly, I caught a glimpse of a flipper up ahead! I ran as fast as I could, but just when I caught up to him, Pete disappeared into the girls' washroom!

*Yikes! I hope it's empty!*

I sucked in my breath and stuck my head into the washroom. My luck held. There was no one inside! Pete was standing under a sink. I darted inside, scooped him up, shoved him under my sweater, and charged out. That's when I bumped into Mrs. Warner, the secretary!

"What were you doing in the girls' washroom?" she asked me sternly.

"I was going to throw up," I said. "I thought it was the boys' washroom." I mixed my answer with a moan.

"Come along to the office if you're not feeling well," she said in a gentler voice.

I bent over so Mrs. Warner wouldn't see the bulge in my sweater and followed her. She pointed to the bench outside the office.

"Sit here and rest for a bit. You're looking red and warm. Perhaps you have a fever."

*I have penguin fever!* I thought.

Mrs. Warner put a large trash can beside me. "In case you feel sick," she said as she felt my forehead. "I have photocopying to do. I'll be in the back room if you need me."

Chapter Six

# Penny!

I sat down to figure out what to do. Pete struggled under my sweater, tickling me.

"Stop wriggling!" I laughed, lifting my sweater. Before I could stop him, Pete hopped right out! I grabbed at him, but he scuttled through the office doors and waddled into the principal's office!

I rushed in after Pete and saw to my relief that the principal, Mr. Fox, wasn't there. Pete hopped onto his chair. Mr. Penguin was the school principal instead of Mr. Fox! I started to laugh, and then I remembered that I was supposed to be sick, so I turned my laugh into a groan.

Mrs. Warner called out from the back room, "Jake, are you all right?"

"I'm fine, don't worry!" I shouted as I grabbed Pete

and put him into the trash can. I pulled off my sweater
and threw it over him. Just as I was smoothing down my
hair, Mr. Fox came down the hallway to his office.

"What are you doing here, Jake?" he asked when he
saw me.

"I'm not feeling very well, sir," I said.

He nodded absentmindedly and went into his office.
The next minute, I heard him exclaim, "What on earth?"

He appeared in the main office and called to Mrs. Warner. "Look at this!" he said, holding up an egg. "Someone's left two eggs on my chair!"

"But no one's been in your office," Mrs. Warner said. "What sort of eggs are they? They don't look much like hens' eggs."

"I'm not sure." Mr. Fox sniffed the air in his office. Then he looked around the room and sniffed again.

"Has there been fish in this room?" he asked.

Mrs. Warner stared at him. "I didn't eat lunch in here today. Besides, I had a salad."

"It's a big mystery, Mrs. Warner."

Mr. Fox shook his head. He went back into his office and shut the door.

Suddenly, I realized that Pete wasn't male after all! He had laid two eggs! I'd have to pick a girl's name!

"How about Penny?" I said into the trash can. I was sure I heard a squawk.

Picking up the trash can, I went up to Mrs. Warner.

"I feel better now. I'll go back to class. Can I borrow the trash can in case I feel sick again?"

"Sure, Jake. Just remember to bring it back after school," she said.

I headed back to class, carrying the trash can with both hands. Everyone was painting except Ryan, who had been waiting anxiously for me. He asked me what had happened. When I told him about the eggs on Mr. Fox's chair, he laughed out loud.

"I wish he'd sat on them!" he said.

"I'll have to get them back," I whispered.

"I'll help you after school," Ryan said.

I was glad when the bell rang and school was over for the day, and for the week.

After all the kids had left the room, Ryan and I took Pete—sorry, Penny—out of the trash can and lowered her into my backpack. Then we went to the office to return the trash can. Mrs. Warner and Mr. Fox weren't around.

While Ryan stayed outside to keep watch, I snuck into Mr. Fox's office for the egg hunt. I spotted them at once. They were sitting in a bowl of paper clips on the desk! I picked up the eggs and slipped them into my pocket. Then Ryan and I made a dash for the door.

"Mr. Fox will think he imagined the little eggs!" I panted.

Max and Brett were waiting for us in the hall. We set off for home together. Ryan kept patting the backpack as we walked. Once, Penny made a noise that sounded like "Yawp!"

"What's that?" Max asked.

"Nothing," I snapped.

"There's something wriggling in there," he insisted.

"Don't be crazy, Max," I said. "And Ryan, leave my backpack alone."

When we got home, I went straight to my room and let Penny out of the backpack. She looked annoyed. I got fresh ice packs for her cooler and put her inside. When I gave her the eggs, she rolled them under her body with her feet and squawked, looking contented.

Chapter Seven

# Max Meets Penny

Mom's car door slammed, and I went down to see what she'd brought home.

"Hi Jake," she said. "Look at all the fish I bought for dinner."

She set the fish pieces on the counter to thaw. When she went upstairs to change, I took the smallest piece and went back up to my room to feed Penny. She ate it up hungrily.

"I'll bring you more later," I told her.

When we sat down for dinner, Max sniffed at his fish and said, "This stinks!" He took a bite and whined, "It's fishy!"

"It *is* fish!" Mom said.

Max poured ketchup all over his fish. Dad and Amanda dug miserably into their fish.

*There'll be lots left behind for Penny!* I thought happily.

"I'll clean up after dinner tonight," I said. "You guys can all go and relax."

"That's nice of you, Jake," Dad said, smiling.

As soon as everyone left the kitchen, I took all the leftover fish up to Penny. She ate it up, ketchup and all. Then she settled back in her cooler, and I went downstairs to clean up as I had promised.

Later that night, I was reading in bed when Max marched into my room. "Okay," he said, arms folded on his chest. "What's going on?"

"What are you talking about?" I asked in an innocent tone.

Max held up one finger. "First, the tuna sandwiches." He held up another finger. "Second, the wiggly backpack." He held up a third finger. "Third, fish for

dinner, and I know you only like it with batter." He held up his little finger. "And fourth, offering to clean up after dinner! What's going on? I want to see what's in your backpack."

"Go ahead and have a look," I said, waving my hand at the empty backpack on the floor. Max picked it up and peered inside. Then he said, "Phew! It stinks! What did you have in there?"

I decided I'd better tell him about Penny, in case I needed his help.

"Look inside the closet," I said.

Max opened the closet door and peered inside. His head whipped right out and he was spluttering. "A *penguin?*"

"Yup! Her name's Penny."

Max reached in gingerly to touch her. "How in the world did you get her?"

Once more, I told the story about Uncle Cyrus's dictionary. Max looked at me scornfully.

"C'mon. I'm not four anymore."

"It's true!" I insisted. "Uncle Cyrus sent me a magic dictionary, that's all."

Max looked at me enviously. "Can I get a penguin, too, then?"

"No! I have enough problems already," I shot back.

"But…" Max started.

"No 'buts,' " I said. "Don't touch my dictionary. Promise."

Max could tell I meant business, and he reluctantly promised.

We heard footsteps in the hallway and shut the closet door just as Dad came in. He read us an exciting story about the Black Knight. When I finally fell asleep, I dreamed about knights on horses chasing hundreds of penguins over the ice.

Chapter Eight

# He Shoots! She Scores!

Saturday mornings are very busy at our house. Amanda goes to gymnastics, and Max and I both have hockey games. Dad coaches my team. Last year he coached Max's.

Our team is on a losing streak. We've lost the last six games, and I wasn't looking forward to losing game seven that day!

Mom, Dad, and I went to watch Max play. His team won. At the arena, it hit me that Penny would enjoy the cold in there. After his game, I told Max to bring Penny with him when he came to watch my game.

We rushed home for a quick snack before my game. Max put Penny in his backpack. She did not wriggle all the way to the rink. I think she liked the car ride.

At the arena, my family stood near the rink, ready to

cheer, while I went to get dressed. Just before we went on the ice, Dad gave the team a final pep talk: "Play your best. You'll be fine."

We looked at the other team, and we didn't feel at all fine. They're in first place, and they're much bigger than we are.

In the first period, we were down by two goals. Dad said, "Don't worry, guys. Just get out on the ice and remember to pass the puck up."

The next period started. Stuart passed to Ryan to pass to Steve. He got a breakaway. The puck went in and we all cheered. I could hear Mom, Max, and Amanda yelling. And I thought I heard a little squawk from Penny.

Then Stuart nailed a rebound, and the score was tied! In the last minute, Steve passed the puck to Ryan, who shot it to Spenser. I was skating really fast along the boards, when I saw something skid onto the ice. It was Penny!

*How did you get out of Max's backpack?* I yelled at her in

my head. I was afraid she would be hurt by the guys'
skates. I zoomed over to her just as the puck came toward
us. Penny reached out a flipper and hit the puck. It went
straight into the net! The goalie dived to stop it, but he
was too late.

As everyone cheered and yelled, I grabbed Penny and stuffed her under my sweater. Luckily, in all the frenzy, no one had noticed her. Then my teammates were on top of me, slapping me on the back and yelling, "Great job, Jake!"

Did I say that our team is called the Mighty Ducks? If they knew who really scored the goal, they'd rename us the Mighty Penguins, instead.

Back at home, and safely in my room, Max said, "I'm sorry I let Penny go, Jake."

"Don't worry about it," I said. "I don't think anyone noticed her, and besides, look what she did. She scored that winning goal."

Max laughed. "You mean it was Penny's shot? We should put her on the team! She could wear a little helmet and a sweater."

I went downstairs for fresh ice packs for Penny, when I heard Mom and Dad talking.

"Are we having steak tonight?" Dad asked hopefully.

"I said Jake could have whatever he liked because he scored the winning goal," came Mom's reply.

"I hope he chose steak," Dad said.

"He picked shrimp," Mom replied.

"What's with this kid and seafood?" Dad grumbled. "He'll grow fins and a tail if he keeps eating like this." He sounded very grumpy.

## Chapter Nine

# Penguin Cop

Penny woke me in the middle of the night by sticking her beak right in my ear.

"Ow! What's your problem?" I hissed at her as I rubbed my ear. Penny waddled to the window and then back again. She wanted to go outside.

"It's one o'clock in the morning!" I turned over and tried to hide my head under my blankets. But then I felt a tug, and then another. I gave up.

"Oh, all right! Come on!" I muttered.

We crept downstairs as quietly as we could. I pulled on my jacket and boots and unlocked the back door. The moon was shining on the snow, and it glistened beautifully.

Penny was happy to be out in the cold. She slid down a

bank in the
backyard and
squawked. My feet
were freezing because I
hadn't put on socks under my
boots. I wasn't enjoying this late-night frolic in the snow.

"We have to go now, Penny."

I tried to pick her up, but she ducked away and headed for the fence. I ran after her. Suddenly, I noticed someone moving in the yard next door. Stunned, I watched as the person crept up to the kitchen window and pried it open. A burglar was trying to break into the Hamiltons' house!

Before I could stop her, Penny had squeezed through

the fence and was running across the snow. She saw the burglar's legs hanging out the window and stuck her beak into one of them. The burglar screamed and fell back into the snow. Penny continued to peck at him. He yelled in terror and tried to push her away.

Then everything happened at once. Lights came on in the Hamiltons' house, and lights flared on in our house. Then I heard the back door open, and Mr. Hamilton yelled out, "Who's there? What's going on out there?"

The burglar had collapsed onto the ground. I went through the fence, grabbed Penny, and ran back home. I thought I'd better let Mr. Hamilton take over now. I raced into my room and dropped Penny into the cooler. Then I heard Dad in the hall.

"What's going on?" he asked. I peeked out into the hall. Dad's hair was standing on end.

"I heard a noise next door. I think Mr. Hamilton needs help," I answered.

Dad ran into my room and looked out the window.

When he saw Mr. Hamilton struggling with a man, he called the police and then rushed over to help. Before long, we heard sirens and squealing tires outside.

Amanda and Mom woke up, and we went out to watch the police take the burglar away. He was moaning and clutching his leg.

"What's wrong with him?" Dad asked Mr. Hamilton.

"I have no idea," Mr. Hamilton said. "He had some crazy story about a bird stabbing him with its beak. Can you believe it?"

Dad laughed. "I don't think the judge will believe him, either," he said.

But I did. I patted Penny, congratulating her on a job well done.

Chapter Ten

# Penny Goes Home

In the morning, Max was mad because he'd slept through the burglar's capture. I had hockey practice at ten o'clock. I told Max to quit grumbling about missing the excitement of the night before.

"I need you to take care of Penny while I'm out," I told him.

"Okay," Max said. "I'll take her to my room and keep her cool."

Dad and I were at the arena until around eleven o'clock. We stopped at the supermarket for milk on the way home. As soon as we got home, I ran upstairs to Max's room. He was lying on the floor, staring at Penny with a worried frown.

"What's wrong?" I asked.

"I think Penny is sick," Max said, glancing up.

I looked at the penguin. She was curled up on her side with her eyes shut.

"Did you give her some tuna?" I asked.

Max nodded and waved a hand at the can on the floor. "She didn't eat it."

"Did you add ketchup?"

He pointed to the bottle of ketchup by his bed.

"She didn't like it," he said. "And she makes this funny noise."

I listened closely. Penny was making a whistling sound when she breathed.

"Do you think she has a cold?" Max asked, stroking Penny gently. I shook my head.

"I don't know, but I sure hope she pulls out of it. She has eggs to hatch."

Just then, Mom called us down to lunch. We put Penny back in her cooler and went downstairs.

"*I'm* cooking dinner tonight," Dad announced as we sat down for lunch. "And it's *steak*."

Mom shook her head and said, "Not tonight, dear. I've got dinner all planned."

"What is it? Does it swim?" Dad asked.

"Well, sort of," said Mom.

Dad groaned. "Tell me the worst. What are we eating *this* time?"

"Squid," said Mom.

"Squid!" Amanda screeched. "Whose sick idea was that?"

"I told Max he could choose tonight," Mom said.

"And he picked squid?" Dad asked. "You boys are getting stranger by the day!"

Penny slept all afternoon. I hoped that the squid from our dinner would perk up her appetite that evening. Just as I'd expected, both Dad and Amanda didn't touch their squid at dinner, so there was plenty left for Penny.

This time, Max offered to clean up. When Mom, Dad, and Amanda had left, we stuffed the leftover squid into our pockets. We raced upstairs and offered it to Penny. She leaned out of the cooler, pecked at the squid, and turned away. We knew then that she was in trouble. But we had no idea how to help her.

Suddenly, we heard Amanda's footsteps in the hallway. I pushed Penny's cooler into the closet and shut the door. Max flung my pajama top over the squid. Amanda barged in without knocking, as usual."What are you guys up to?" she asked.

"Nothing," I said, trying to look cool.

"Your room stinks!" Amanda said. "Are you keeping dirty socks in here, Jake?"

"Yup! Lots of them," I said. "And dirty pants, too."

"You're gross!" she exclaimed. "And you should pick up your clothes!"

She lifted the pajamas with her foot and screamed when she saw the squid.

"Why is this stuff here? I knew you guys didn't like squid! What's going on here?"

Max and I looked at each other glumly and nodded. It was time to tell her about Penny.

Of course, Amanda didn't believe us.

"What are you talking about? Have you gone crazy?" she asked, her hands on her hips.

I opened the closet door and pulled out the cooler. Amanda's jaw dropped. She fell to her knees and stroked Penny.

"Oh, she's so cute," she said. Then she looked up and said, "Okay, out with it. Where did you guys steal her from?"

"Amanda, Uncle Cyrus sent Jake a magic dictionary! Penny just popped up in the closet when Jake was reading about penguins," Max yelled.

"But she's not feeling well, Amanda," I said. "I'm getting worried about her."

"Can you help her, Amanda? She's trying to hatch her eggs," added Max.

"If you're telling me the truth," Amanda said thoughtfully, "I'll bet she's homesick. She looks sad. You'll have to send her back to wherever she came from."

"But I don't know how to do that," I said.

"Well, what did you do to make her appear?" Amanda asked.

"I was just looking at a picture of a penguin in the dictionary, and all of a sudden, she was there, in my closet!" I replied.

"Well, do that again, then," Amanda said.

I opened the dictionary to the right page and read about penguins. Nothing happened.

"You must have done something else," Amanda said. "Think hard. What did you do?"

"Let's take her out of the cooler and leave her in the closet with the door shut," Max said. We did that, and I carefully reread the definition of a penguin. We opened the closet door. Penny was still inside.

"You'll have to concentrate," Amanda said. "Try to remember exactly what you did."

I closed my eyes and thoroughly went over everything

that I'd done that day.

"I've got it!" I yelled. "I tapped on the picture when I first saw it! That must be it!"

"Try it, then!" Max said.

I tapped on the picture of the penguin in the dictionary. Penny didn't move.

"Wait a minute," Amanda said. "You tapped *once* to bring her here. Maybe you have to tap *twice* to send her back."

I tapped the picture once, and then tapped again. We checked the closet. It was empty! Penny was gone. The eggs had vanished, too.

"Wow!" Amanda and Max shouted together.

I looked sadly at Penny's picture in the dictionary. Then I whistled in surprise.

"What's the matter?" Amanda asked.

"The eggs!" I said. "They weren't in the picture before, but now look!"

In the picture, there
were two little eggs
sitting beside Penny.

"Wow!" Amanda said.
"That means Penny *did*
make it safely back."

"Super!" Max exclaimed.

"What an amazing dictionary!" I said.

Mom and Dad were having coffee in the den.

"What's for dinner tomorrow, honey?" Dad asked.

"Guess," Mom teased.

"Whale? Shark?"

"Wrong, wrong."

"Oysters? Stingray?"

"Wrong again. It's what you've been asking for all week."

"Steak?" Dad asked happily. "Great! And I guess you'll
get fish for the boys?" he added.

"Steak's just fine!" Max and I said together.

## Little Penguin Fact Sheet

▶ Penguins don't look like birds, but they are actually flightless birds that happen to be excellent swimmers. They virtually "fly" through the water!

▶ Little penguins (also called blue penguins or fairy penguins) are the world's smallest penguins. They weigh just over two pounds and reach a height of about fourteen inches.

▶ They live near the sea in Australia and New Zealand.

▶ In New Zealand, their Maori name is *korora*.

▶ They dig burrows on land for their nests and lay two eggs in the spring.

▶ Rats and weasels are their main enemies.

▶ They like to eat fish and shellfish.

▶ They can live as long as twenty years.

For more information on penguins, check out some of the amazing penguin websites on the Internet. Try going to a search engine and typing in the word *penguin* to see what you can find!

# Using a Dictionary

You become a better reader and writer when you learn new words. Words become yours when you understand what they mean and use them in your writing and discussions.

Use a dictionary to look up any words in this book that you don't understand. You might want to start your own personal list of new words in a journal, or in a file in your computer. First, write down the definition of the word. Then use the word in a short sentence. The next time you write a short story, or an essay, try to use new words that you have learned. You will be amazed at how quickly you can expand your vocabulary this way.